Original title:
The Eternal Petal

Copyright © 2024 Swan Charm
All rights reserved.

Author: Johan Kirsipuu
ISBN HARDBACK: 978-9908-1-1957-1
ISBN PAPERBACK: 978-9908-1-1958-8
ISBN EBOOK: 978-9908-1-1959-5

Traces of Whispers in Buds

In quiet hush, the petals sigh,
New dreams awaken, shyly spry.
Soft whispers linger, secrets held,
In tender blooms, life gently swelled.

Each bud a tale of moments past,
Fragile hopes that bloom so fast.
In twilight's glow, they softly gleam,
A silent witness to every dream.

Timelessness Woven in Blossom's Dance

Beneath the sun, the flowers sway,
In nature's rhythm, they find their way.
A dance that speaks of days gone by,
Their fragrant laughter fills the sky.

With every breeze, they weave their tune,
A symphony beneath the moon.
Each blossom's turn, a fleeting glance,
In twilight's breath, we join the dance.

A Symphony of the Ageless Blossom

In gardens lush, a chorus sings,
Of timeless joys that nature brings.
The petals paint a vibrant hue,
An ageless song so fresh and new.

With every bloom, life's cycle flows,
A melody that softly grows.
Together in this vibrant throng,
They share the story, sweet and strong.

In the Embrace of Nature's Continuum

Amidst the branches, life unfolds,
In every petal, wisdom holds.
Nature's hands, they guide the way,
In every dawn, a brand new day.

The roots entwined, the skies above,
A bond unbroken, purest love.
In whispers shared, we come alive,
Within the blooms, our spirits thrive.

Harvesting Dreams in Petal-Laden Fields

In fields of gold, dreams take flight,
Where petals dance in morning light.
Each whisper soft, a promise made,
In the embrace of nature's jade.

Underneath the azure sky,
We gather hopes as time slips by.
With every bloom, our spirits soar,
Each moment rich, we ask for more.

The sun dips low, the shadows blend,
In fragrant realms, our hearts ascend.
Together we weave our tapestry,
Of love and laughter, wild and free.

As twilight falls, colors ignite,
In stillness found, we chase the night.
With every dream, a seed we sow,
Tomorrow's warmth, a radiant glow.

So let us dance, beneath the trees,
In this haven, we find our peace.
Harvesting dreams, we stand as one,
Petal-laden fields, our journey begun.

Serenade of the Flowering Past

In the quiet of twilight's grace,
Ghosts of laughter fill the space.
Memories bloom like fragrant flowers,
Whispering tales of golden hours.

Each petal holds a story dear,
A serenade we long to hear.
Soft echoes of a youthful song,
In the garden where we belong.

Beneath the boughs of ancient trees,
Dreams woven in the evening breeze.
With every rustle, hearts awaken,
Threads of time that can't be shaken.

As night unfolds its velvet sheet,
We trace the paths of love's heartbeat.
In shadows cast by lantern's glow,
The flowering past begins to flow.

So stand with me, as stars appear,
In this moment, we'll shed a tear.
For all the dreams that brightly shone,
In the serenade, we're never alone.

The Resilience of Fragile Colors

In a world where colors fade,
Fragile hues are not afraid.
With every storm that bends and breaks,
A vibrant heart, the soul awakes.

Petals fall but spirits rise,
Embracing change, we touch the skies.
Through all the trials, shadows cast,
Resilience blooms; we find the past.

Each brush of wind, a gentle guide,
The dance of life, our hearts abide.
In shades of hope, we reappear,
With every tear, we shed the fear.

Amongst the ruins, beauty shines,
In every crack, the sun defines.
A tapestry of hues unfolds,
The resilience of fragile souls.

So let us cherish every hue,
In every loss, we start anew.
For life's a canvas, bold and bright,
A masterpiece in shadows' light.

In the Shade of Forever Green

Beneath the boughs, we find our rest,
In the shade where dreams are blessed.
With whispers soft, the leaves confer,
A serenade that stirs the air.

Time slows down, as moments flow,
In nature's grasp, we come to know.
Each rustling leaf a story told,
In the embrace of shades so bold.

The dance of light through branches plays,
A fleeting glimpse of sunny rays.
Amongst the roots, our secrets lie,
In the shade, we learn to fly.

With every breath, the world feels right,
In harmony, we find our light.
For in this haven, dreams convene,
In the shade of forever green.

So linger here, in warmth and peace,
Let worries fade, let troubles cease.
For life unfolds in nature's scheme,
In the shade, we harvest dreams.

A Leaf's Lament in Stillness

Once green and vibrant, I sway,
Caught in a quiet decay.
Memories of sunlit days,
Fading in a still display.

Whispers captured on the breeze,
Stories told among the trees.
Each flutter, a quiet sigh,
Yearning for the azure sky.

I fell from branches once so high,
Now rest where the shadows lie.
Crimson hues in autumn's chill,
The end, yet I linger still.

Rain will wash my colors bright,
As night turns to morning light.
Yet in my silence, I find peace,
A gentle sigh, a sweet release.

For every season has its song,
A cycle where we all belong.
Though stillness wraps me in its guise,
A leaf's lament shall never die.

Colors of a Never-Fading Dream

In twilight's embrace, hues collide,
Imagined worlds where dreams abide.
Each shade a whisper of the night,
Painting the stars with soft delight.

Golden rays kiss the horizon,
Where echoes of laughter rise and shine.
In the realm where wishes soar,
Colors dance forevermore.

Violet skies that stretch so wide,
A canvas where hopes reside.
Every brushstroke, a heartbeat's tune,
Chasing wonders beneath the moon.

Time cannot dim this radiant glow,
In every shade, the heart will know.
A tapestry woven with care,
Colors bloom, and joys ensnare.

Amidst the dreams where spirits play,
In vivid shades, we twirl and sway.
Forever etched in memory's stream,
The colors of a never-fading dream.

Buds Beneath the Celestial Sphere

Awake beneath the midnight sky,
Buds emerge with a gentle sigh.
Each promise wrapped in dew's embrace,
Yearning for warmth in this vast space.

Stars whisper secrets, soft and clear,
Guiding the blooms as spring draws near.
Colors bloom in radiant light,
Challenging the long, cold night.

Petals unfurling, shy and sweet,
Find their courage, feel the heat.
Underneath the celestial dome,
Buds awaken, find their home.

Moonlit shadows dance in thrill,
Calling forth life with every will.
Nature's chorus lifts its voice,
In the buds, we all rejoice.

To grow, to reach, to grasp the air,
Beneath the stars, we shed our care.
Each blossom born in whispered cheer,
A promise held beneath the sphere.

The Cycle Without Conclusion

As seasons turn, we spin and sway,
Life unfolds in its grand ballet.
Every ending marks a start,
The cycle flows within the heart.

Fleeting moments weave the thread,
In laughter shared, in tears once shed.
What begins must also cease,
Yet in the pause, we find our peace.

Days turn to nights, and nights to days,
In endless loops, we dance in praise.
The sun will rise, then fade away,
Yet memories linger, come what may.

Every dawn brings hope anew,
Yet shadows linger, ever true.
Though paths may twist and turn askew,
The cycle spins—a constant cue.

Embrace the flow, the ebbing tide,
In every phase, we must abide.
For in this dance without refrain,
The cycle lives, despite the pain.

Petals Echoing Through Ages

In the soft light of dawn's first kiss,
Petals whisper secrets of the past.
They dance in the breeze, a fleeting bliss,
Echoes of moments, forever cast.

Each bloom a tale that time has spun,
Colors fading yet bright in dreams.
The journey continues, never done,
In gardens of hope, where beauty gleams.

Gardens of Shimmering Endurance

In quiet corners where shadows play,
Petals shimmer with morning dew.
Each fragile beauty, a bold display,
Enduring storms, yet always true.

Roots intertwine like stories told,
In whispered winds, resilience sings.
Gardens of life, both brave and bold,
Unfurl the love that nature brings.

The Unseen Embrace of Nature's Bloom

In the heart of silence, blooms awake,
Petals reach for the sky so clear.
With every heartbeat, life they stake,
The unseen magic of warmth draws near.

They cradle the dreams of those who wait,
In tender hues, they weave their charm.
Nature's embrace, a calming fate,
In every fragrance, a gentle balm.

A Tapestry Woven in Fragrance

Threads of scent wrap the wandering soul,
Each petal a stitch in the grand design.
In gardens where time has no control,
Fragrance lingers, a soft divine.

Woven together, stories unfold,
In every hue, a tale to share.
Their beauty timeless, vibrant and bold,
A tapestry blooming in fragrant air.

Blooming in the Realm of Eternity

Amidst the stars, a flower gleams,
Its petals dance in endless dreams.
Whispers of love in fragrant air,
A timeless bond that none can tear.

In shadows cast by ancient trees,
It sways gently with the breeze.
Each moment captured, forever bright,
Illuminated by celestial light.

With roots that reach through space and time,
This sacred garden, truly sublime.
In quiet corners, secrets lie,
As blooms unfurl to greet the sky.

Through distant realms, its essence flows,
In colors soft, a magic grows.
Transcending boundaries, it will thrive,
Eternity's breath, keeping it alive.

An Ode to Unfading Beauty

In twilight's glow, a vision stands,
With grace adorned, it understands.
The gentle touch of fleeting grace,
An echo held in time and space.

Upon the canvas of the earth,
A testament of vibrant worth.
Through seasons' change, it does not fade,
A portrait of life, serenely made.

With every glance, a story told,
Of love and warmth that never grows old.
A shining beacon, forever clear,
Its message lingers, ever near.

In gardens wide, it finds its home,
In every heart, it dares to roam.
A beauty born to light the soul,
Throughout the ages, it will unroll.

Tides of Color, Waves of Time

The oceans rise with hues divine,
A symphony of shades that shine.
Each wave a stroke of nature's hand,
On the canvas of this vibrant land.

As sunsets merge with dawn's embrace,
Colors dance in soft, fluid grace.
A tapestry woven through the air,
Reflecting dreams, light as a prayer.

In stillness found upon the shore,
Echoes of beauty, we explore.
The rhythms of life, a gentle rhyme,
In tides of color, waves of time.

With every crest, a moment shared,
In fleeting whispers, love is bared.
A vibrant story that unfolds,
In the heart's canvas, life beholds.

Vestiges of Bloom in the Wind

In softest sighs, the petals fall,
Whispers of spring's enchanting call.
Through the branches, breezes play,
Carrying scents of a brighter day.

Once vibrant blooms now scatter wide,
Carried aloft on nature's tide.
Each burst of color, a fleeting kiss,
In memory's heart, we find our bliss.

Amongst the remnants of what has passed,
Lies beauty deep, forever cast.
In gentle breezes, echoes remain,
The sweet refrain of joy and pain.

Though time may steal the brightest hue,
In every moment, it feels brand new.
Vestiges linger, soft and kind,
In the dance of leaves, love we'll find.

Petals of Perpetual Dreams

In the whispers of the night,
Moonlight dances on the stream.
Stars awaken, shining bright,
Carrying tales of sweet dreams.

Underneath the willow's sway,
A breeze carries soft delight.
Petals drift and gently play,
Guiding hearts with pure respite.

Among the blooms, colors blaze,
Echoing laughter's soft call.
Every fragrance weaves a maze,
As memories begin to sprawl.

With each heartbeat, hopes arise,
Tales of love softly grow.
In this realm, no goodbyes,
Where every dream finds its flow.

In the twilight's tender glow,
Whispers fade into the dream.
Petals dance to and fro,
As we float on wisdom's stream.

Fading Light of a Sunlit Blossom

As daylight wanes, shadows creep,
A sunlit blossom sighs low.
In twilight's grasp, secrets sleep,
Telling tales only they know.

The garden glows in amber hue,
With petals kissed by soft light.
Fading hues of gold and blue,
Embrace the coming of night.

In the silence, whispers blend,
Nature's serenade takes flight.
As colors shift, dreams transcend,
Holding on till morning's light.

Within each bloom, histories lie,
Moments cherished, forever.
Their fragrance calls, a sweet sigh,
Binding hearts, a gentle tether.

With every dusk, life renews,
In shadows, beauty refrains.
Fading light in vibrant hues,
Carrying whispers like chains.

Chronicles of a Blooming Soul

In the garden of the mind,
Petals open, truths reveal.
Life's adventures intertwined,
Crafting stories that we feel.

Every leaf a page of grace,
Speaking softly to the heart.
In each flower, a time and space,
Reminding us of our part.

Beneath the sun's warm embrace,
Dreams are nurtured, hopes take flight.
In this serene, sacred place,
Every shade glows with pure light.

Memories bloom, sometimes fade,
Yet each petal leaves a trace.
In the twilight, dreams are laid,
In the garden's sweet embrace.

With every season, new tales spun,
A blooming soul finds its way.
Under the ever-watching sun,
Chronicles of love on display.

In the Garden of Forever

Beneath the arch of skies so blue,
Lies the garden's gentle grace.
With every dream that we pursue,
Timeless love, in this place.

Petals whisper secret lore,
Each bloom a promise held tight.
Amongst these flowers, we explore,
Chasing shadows touched by light.

In every fragrance, stories flow,
Binding hearts in soft embrace.
Through the seasons, love will grow,
Defining time, our sacred space.

With pathways planted, seeds of hope,
Guiding journeys hand in hand.
In this garden, we shall cope,
Finding peace where dreams withstand.

In the twilight, stars will weep,
For the moments we hold dear.
In the garden, forever sleep,
Where love glistens, pure and clear.

Remnants of a Silken Blossom

In the garden where dreams bloom,
Petals whisper of days gone by,
Fleeting shadows of fragrant light,
Echoes sweet as a lullaby.

Softly cradled in evening's glow,
The remnants dance upon the air,
Fragile threads of a past embrace,
Carried lightly without a care.

In twilight's brush, a memory stirs,
Silken secrets wrapped in dew,
Each sigh of wind tells a story,
Of love that once brightly grew.

With every breeze, their beauty fades,
Yet hope hangs on with tender grace,
In the heart where the silken rests,
Legacy in a timeless space.

So here's to blossoms that will fade,
In their silence, a truth draws near,
For within the remnants of their charm,
Lies the essence of what we hold dear.

Enigma of the Everlasting Leaf

A single leaf upon the floor,
Holds tales of seasons past,
Whispers of wind and the sun's embrace,
In nature's grip, forever cast.

Dancing shadows around the tree,
Flickering thoughts in the breeze,
What secrets lie within its veins,
In the hush of rustling leaves?

Green to gold, then crisp and brown,
Each change a story, a song,
A cycle that binds us to the earth,
A reminder we all belong.

In the labyrinth of time's vast maze,
The leaf persists through joy and grief,
An enigma woven by nature's hand,
An ode to life, the everlasting leaf.

So ponder now this fragile tale,
Of resilience and endless flight,
For within each leaf that tumbles down,
Lies the heart of nature's might.

Unraveling Nature's Timekeeper

In the forest where silence reigns,
Time weaves through branches high,
Softly ticking like a heartbeat,
As the moments pass us by.

Watch the shadows stretch and fold,
With the sun's warm, golden trace,
Each second wrapped in tender light,
Nature's breath, a timeless space.

Rainfall glistens on the leaves,
Marking memories in each drop,
The rhythms of life intertwined,
In a dance that never stops.

As twilight drapes its gentle cloak,
Stars awaken, flickering bright,
The heavens quilt the earth below,
In the hush of the approaching night.

So stand and listen to the pulse,
Feel the whispers of the trees,
For nature's timekeeper breathes with us,
Entwined in infinite ease.

The Flute of the Wildflower Choir

Amid the fields where colors blend,
Wildflowers hum a sweet refrain,
Petals flutter, soft and bright,
In harmony with nature's pain.

The flute of dreams plays soft and low,
Each note a story, rich and clear,
Carried on the gentle breeze,
A melody we long to hear.

Daisies, violets in the throng,
Join the chorus of the wild,
Their voices rise in pure delight,
A symphony, nature's child.

As dusk approaches, shadows lengthen,
The choir softens, yet it stays,
In the heart of every blossom,
Resides the magic of their praise.

So linger long within this space,
Where wildflowers sing to the night,
In the flute of the wildflower choir,
Find a world of pure delight.

The Poise of Unyielding Flora

In gardens bright, they stand so tall,
Roots grip the earth, defying all.
Petals soft in the gentle breeze,
Their silent strength brings us to ease.

Through storms they sway, yet never break,
Colors bold, for beauty's sake.
Each bloom a tale of grit and grace,
In nature's dance, they find their place.

Witness the fight in each fierce bloom,
Against the shadows, they consume.
With open hearts, they claim the sun,
In every struggle, they have won.

Through seasons harsh, they grow anew,
In every shade, a vibrant hue.
The poise they wear, a sight to see,
In quiet strength, they remain free.

Unyielding flora, brave and bright,
In darkest hours, their spirits light.
A testament to life's refrain,
Through every loss, they rise again.

In the Light of Evermore

Beneath a sky of endless dreams,
Where twilight falls and softly gleams.
Each star a wish, or so they say,
In the light of evermore, we stay.

Whispers echo in the cool night air,
Promises held in hearts laid bare.
Moments captured in tender glow,
In the light of evermore, we grow.

Time flows softly like a gentle stream,
Carving paths through the seams of dreams.
Memory dances in moonlit rays,
In the light of evermore, it stays.

With every dawn, new colors shine,
Rich tapestries of space and time.
Bound by the hope that love can bring,
In the light of evermore, we sing.

So let us wander through this expanse,
Where shadows fade and spirits dance.
Together we'll weave a tale untold,
In the light of evermore, we're bold.

Threads of Life Interwoven

In the fabric of life, threads intertwine,
Stories woven, yours and mine.
Each strand a journey, rich and deep,
In every heart, memories to keep.

Tapestries bright with laughter and tears,
Each moment stitched, through all the years.
Colors blend in a vibrant swirl,
Threads of life in a graceful twirl.

Connections made with every touch,
Binding souls that mean so much.
Through trials faced, we find our way,
Threads of life that never fray.

A gentle hand to stitch anew,
In every hue, a love that's true.
Together we weave our destinies,
Threads of life, like autumn leaves.

So cherish each link, each bond sincere,
For they are what we hold most dear.
In every thread, a story flows,
Threads of life, as the heartbeat grows.

Songs of the Ageless Blossom

In gardens where the wild winds blow,
The ageless blossoms start to show.
Each petal whispers tales of old,
In vibrant hues, and heartbeats bold.

From dormant seeds to skies above,
They sing the songs of life and love.
Through time and trials, they still remain,
In the face of storm, they will sustain.

A symphony of scents exchanged,
In every note, our hearts are changed.
Together they dance in morning light,
Songs of the ageless, pure and bright.

In every rustle, secrets shared,
A melody of hearts that cared.
With roots that dig through soil and stone,
Songs of the ageless, never alone.

So let their chorus fill the air,
In every breath, a moment rare.
For life, like blossoms, always grows,
In songs of the ageless, beauty flows.

Timeless Blooms Beneath the Stars

In gardens where the shadows creep,
Petals whisper, secrets they keep.
Night's embrace, a tranquil balm,
In moonlit grace, their colors calm.

Stars ignite the darkened skies,
While blooms reflect their soft replies.
In every bud, the dreams arise,
Timeless blooms where beauty lies.

The breeze carries scents of lore,
Ancient tales from yesteryear's door.
Each flower's breath, a soft refrain,
In twilight's hush, they sing again.

Beneath these stars, the world is still,
Nature's wonder, a sacred thrill.
In silence, they dance, ever free,
Timeless blooms in harmony.

As dawn approaches, light will blend,
Nature's canvas, never to end.
With each new day, they will renew,
Timeless blooms, forever true.

The Lifeline of a Fragile Leaf

A single leaf hangs by a thread,
Caught in whispers of words unsaid.
In gentle winds it sways and bends,
A lifeline that nature transcends.

Through storms and sun, it learns to cling,
Embracing life, the joy it brings.
Each vein a story, etched in green,
Of all the places it has been.

With morning dew, it glistens bright,
A fragile dance, a fleeting sight.
Yet in its heart, it knows the way,
To thrive anew with each new day.

When autumn calls with chilly breath,
It knows the cycle, life and death.
Each flutter down becomes a sign,
That life persists, in love divine.

So cherish all the simple things,
The fragile leaf, the joy it brings.
In every rustle, listen close,
For in its sigh, the world's a prose.

Beneath Velvet Skies, They Flourish

Beneath the velvet skies so deep,
In twilight's heart, the dreams they keep.
Stars twinkle close, a guiding light,
In this realm where day meets night.

They rise and stretch, the flowers bold,
In hues of crimson, blue, and gold.
Each petal sighs, in stillness blooms,
A symphony of sweet perfumes.

Amidst the hush, whispers resound,
In every corner, life is found.
Beneath the stars, they weave and spin,
In nature's magic, the dance begins.

With every blush of dawn's first glow,
They greet the sun, all aglow.
In velvet skies, they lose their fears,
Embracing joy through all the years.

And as the night wraps them in peace,
In nature's arms, their joys increase.
Beneath the velvet skies they thrive,
In gentle whispers, they come alive.

Endless Seasons of Quiet Beauty

In whispers soft, the seasons change,
A dance of time, a lovely range.
From spring's first kiss to winter's breath,
Each moment sweet, beyond all death.

Blossoms bloom in colors bright,
Underneath the warming light.
Then leaves turn gold, a graceful bow,
In autumn's glow, they take their vow.

Beneath the snow, the silence hums,
In quietude, where stillness comes.
Yet life awaits in dreams held tight,
For spring returns, a hopeful sight.

Cycles spin as life goes on,
In nature's heart, we find our song.
Each season brings its own delight,
In endless beauty, day and night.

So let us watch as time unfolds,
In every hue, the earth beholds.
For in these seasons, we find grace,
Endless beauty, our shared space.

Portrait of an Unforgotten Stem

In the garden where memories bloom,
A stem stands tall, defying the gloom.
Whispers of time in the gentle breeze,
Holding secrets of love and peace.

With petals faded but colors bright,
It weaves tales in the softest light.
A testament to all that it bore,
Life's fleeting dance, yet wanting more.

Rooted deep, it braves the storm,
Through thunderous skies, it keeps warm.
Each leaf a story, a life retold,
In silence, its strength forever bold.

Seasons change and shadows cast,
Yet the stem remains, defying the past.
In every dawn, it finds new grace,
A portrait conceived in nature's embrace.

So here it stands, proud and free,
An emblem of what we may be.
In the heart of the garden's fate,
An unforgotten stem, forever great.

Hymn of the Ageless Garden

In the hearth of blossoms, silence sings,
Beneath the shade where harmony clings.
A chorus of colors, so rich and bright,
The ageless garden in morning light.

With roots that entwine in earth's embrace,
Life weaves a rhythm, a sacred space.
Each flower a note in a timeless song,
Echoing truths that have lingered long.

Whispers of breezes through branches sway,
Telling the tales of the night and day.
In every petal, a memory clear,
A hymn of the garden, forever dear.

Under the skies with stars so bold,
Secrets of love and warmth retold.
In fragrant blooms, the heart can find,
A place woven deep in the soul and mind.

As seasons dance in their endless waltz,
The garden remains, devoid of faults.
It thrives in moments, in laughter and tears,
A hymn of life that transcends years.

The Luminous Petals of Affection

In twilight's glow, soft petals gleam,
A delicate dance, like a tender dream.
They flutter gently on the evening air,
Whispers of love, lifted with care.

Each hue a promise, a warmth so deep,
In the luminous light where sorrows seep.
A fragrance that lingers from rose to vine,
In gardens where hearts either break or entwine.

When shadows fall, they do not fade,
For love's true essence is never betrayed.
With each falling petal, a story unfolds,
Of warmth and connection, in silence, it holds.

In every bloom, a memory we find,
A tapestry woven, a bond that binds.
Through joyful moments and trials we share,
The luminous petals of affection declare.

So gather these treasures, hold them near,
For in every petal, there's laughter and cheer.
In the heart of the garden, let love be the guide,
Through luminous petals, forever abide.

When Seasons Embrace Forever

When springtime meets the warmth of the sun,
A gentle embrace, a dance just begun.
The flowers awaken, unfold with grace,
In nature's arms, they find their place.

Summer dances in fragrant bloom,
Colorful whispers dispel all gloom.
In sun-kissed hues, the moments unite,
As day surrenders softly to night.

Autumn arrives with a crisp embrace,
Transforming the garden, painting each space.
With leaves that fall like a lover's sigh,
The beauty of change, not a reason to cry.

Winter blankets the world in white,
A tranquil hush wraps day into night.
Yet under the frost, life quietly waits,
For spring's soft return and love that elates.

So cherish the cycles, each passing phase,
For in every season, life finds new ways.
When seasons embrace, as they always do,
The heart of the garden remains ever true.

Whispers of Timeless Blooms

In gardens where the shadows play,
The petals dance at end of day.
Their colors speak of tales untold,
In whispers soft, their truths unfold.

The breeze carries a sweet refrain,
Of love and loss, of joy and pain.
A fragrant lullaby it sings,
As twilight wraps its gentle wings.

Beneath the stars, they dream out loud,
In silken folds, beneath the shroud.
Each bloom a story, rich and bright,
Illuminated by moonlight.

The dewdrops cling, like tears of time,
Reflecting life's sweet, perfect rhyme.
In every hue, a moment stays,
In tranquil silence, the heart obeys.

As night descends, they seem to sigh,
Yet in their sleep, they never die.
For in the dawn, they'll rise anew,
With whispers of a world in view.

Fragrance in the Twilight

The sun dips low, the sky ablaze,
A canvas painted, a lasting gaze.
In gardens hushed, the shadows creep,
While fragrant blooms begin to weep.

The evening air, so soft and sweet,
Embraces blossoms, kissed by heat.
A symphony of scents arise,
As night unveils the starry skies.

Each petal holds a secret thought,
A memory of love once wrought.
In twilight's calm, their colors blend,
Tales of seasons that never end.

The moonlight bathes the world in grace,
As flowers find their sacred space.
In silver glow, they gently sway,
A fragrant sigh at end of day.

In every breath, a story glows,
Of fleeting time and love's soft throes.
In twilight's arms, they softly bloom,
Their fragrance filling every room.

A Blossom's Infinite Journey

From seed to sprout, a tale unfolds,
In nature's hands, their fate is told.
Each petal whispers to the sky,
A dream that sways, a wish that flies.

Through storms and sun, they learn to thrive,
In every trial, they come alive.
With roots so deep, they stand so tall,
In every season, they give their all.

The honeybees come, a buzzing song,
In gardens where they all belong.
With each embrace, life's thread is spun,
A journey shared, two hearts as one.

As autumn's chill begins to bite,
They hold the colors of pure light.
In fading warmth, their essence stays,
A blossom's love, through all arrays.

In winter's chill, when all seems bare,
They dream of spring, the warmth to share.
For in the cycle, they find their way,
A timeless dance, come what may.

Petals of Perpetual Grace

In morning's blush, the petals gleam,
A gentle start, like waking dreams.
They stretch and yawn in soft sunlight,
Inviting all to share their light.

With every drop of dew that falls,
They gather hope, answering calls.
In vibrant hues, they paint the day,
In petals soft, they find their play.

As breezes weave through branches high,
They sway and twirl, embracing sky.
In every moment, grace abounds,
A dance of joy that knows no bounds.

When twilight wraps the world in gold,
Their secrets whispered, tales retold.
In night's embrace, they softly rest,
A testament to nature's best.

Through seasons old, they never fade,
In every heart, their marks are laid.
The petals live, and love remains,
In whispers soft, their beauty reigns.

Legends Silhouetted on a Blooming Canvas

In whispers soft, the legends stride,
Their tales are woven wide and side.
A blooming canvas, colors collide,
In each heart, a mystery bides.

With every stroke, the past reborn,
Embracing dreams in daylight's adorn.
A shadow dance as daylight's worn,
In twilight's glow, hopes are sworn.

The brush of fate, a gentle hands,
On petals bright, the future stands.
Each color vibrant, blooms like bands,
Their fragrances through time expands.

The artist's sigh, the silence gleams,
In shades of joy, in hues of dreams.
A tapestry of life redeems,
In every heart, a story streams.

With legends etched, we watch and learn,
In every twist, our passions burn.
On blooming canvases, we turn,
Creating paths where dreams return.

The Lifelong Journey of a Single Petal

A single petal, soft and frail,
Embarks on journeys, tales to unveil.
Through sun and rain, it dares to sail,
On breezes wild, it tells its tale.

From budding bloom to ground below,
It whispers secrets of how to grow.
With every gust, it sways and flows,
In nature's hand, it learns to glow.

The seasons change, the world spins fast,
Yet on this path, the petal's cast.
In moments bright, in shadows vast,
It finds its peace, it holds steadfast.

Through tangled weeds and sunlit fields,
Each day, a new surprise it yields.
In every breath, the earth reveals,
A petal's heart, its truth concealed.

Life's fleeting glance, a precious gift,
With every moment, it starts to lift.
On timeless winds, it learns to drift,
A lifelong journey, love's sweet rift.

Marvels of a Flourishing Horizon

Beyond the hills, the horizon glows,
A marvel found where the wild grass grows.
With every sunrise, a promise flows,
In nature's arms, wonder bestows.

Among the fields, the colors shift,
In shades of green, the spirits lift.
A tapestry where dreams are rife,
In whispers soft, the morning's gift.

The vibrant blooms awaken sights,
In fluttering wings, in joyful flights.
The canvas broad, in dazzling lights,
Where every heart finds its delights.

As shadows dance, the day turns gold,
With every story waiting to be told.
In gentle breezes, the future unfolds,
A flourishing horizon, strong and bold.

In twilight's embrace, the stars emerge,
Where whispered dreams and passions surge.
A timeless realm, where hearts converge,
In marvels vast, our souls converge.

Tides of Fragrance in the Ether

The tides of fragrance sweep the land,
In gentle waves, a soft demand.
They carry secrets, the heart's command,
In whispers sweet, they firmly stand.

With every breeze, a story sways,
Of blooms and nights, of sunlit plays.
In every breath, the magic stays,
As life unfolds in fragrant ways.

From petals pure, the scents arise,
In floral notes, where beauty lies.
The earth's embrace, a sweet surprise,
In nature's arms, our spirits rise.

With seasons turning, scents evolve,
Each drop of dew, a mystery to solve.
In every space, our dreams revolve,
In tides of fragrance, hearts dissolve.

So let us drift on fragrant seas,
In harmonies with every breeze.
With open hearts, we find our peace,
In tides of fragrance, never cease.

Reflections of Nature's Peddler

In twilight's glow, the shadows fall,
A whispering breeze, nature's call.
With petals bright, the colors merge,
A dance of life at the edge of urge.

Through fields of gold, the wanderer roams,
Gathering treasures, a tapestry of homes.
Each bloom a story, in silence they speak,
In harmony's cradle, both strong and weak.

The sun's warm kiss on dewy leaves,
A canvas alive, where the heart believes.
Nature's peddler walks the line,
Weaving magic in every vine.

With the rustle of grass and the songs of trees,
Life's quiet beauty dances in the breeze.
Every moment, a gift to hold,
Reflections of wonders, silently bold.

As Time Weaves Through Lace Petals

Through hands of time, each thread is spun,
A tapestry bright, a race never run.
In the garden of dreams, where moments blend,
Lace petals whisper, a story to send.

With gentle grace, the hours strip,
Each second a petal, time's slow trip.
In the cradle of dusk, shadows play,
Weaving through moments, they softly sway.

As light filters down, the world within,
Each dew drop glimmers, where dreams begin.
The scent of roses, a sweet perfume,
Echoes of time in the evening bloom.

Through thorny paths, where memories hide,
Love's gentle whispers and echoes abide.
In nature's embrace, we find our place,
As time weaves through, leaving its trace.

Stories Carved in Floral Textures

In gardens lush, stories unwind,
Floral textures, nature defined.
Each petal curves with tales to tell,
In silent whispers, they cast their spell.

From roots that anchor, to blooms that soar,
Nature's own book, forevermore.
Colors of life, in vibrant hues,
Embrace the heart, in morning dews.

The sun dips low, shadows play,
While floral tales dance the day away.
Each blade of grass holds secrets deep,
In the heart of the earth, a promise to keep.

As bees hum softly, the breeze will sigh,
Through petals and leaves, the stories fly.
In every blossom, a legacy pressed,
Carved in the earth, nature's behest.

Paintbrush of the Eternal Bloom

With strokes of light, the dawn awakes,
A canvas alive, where beauty breaks.
Each color spills like laughter and tears,
A masterpiece crafted through all the years.

In the painter's heart, a garden takes flight,
Beneath the sun's glow, in soft twilight.
A brush in hand, the artist knows,
Each flower's story, where magic flows.

The purple's whisper, the yellow's cheer,
Each petal speaks, so crystal clear.
Ink of the earth in colors divine,
Paintbrush of bloom, in love's design.

With every stroke, the soul takes shape,
In floral hues, the heart escapes.
To linger in gardens where time stands still,
Eternal blooms feed the spirit's will.

Memory Lane in a Petal's Caress

In the garden where echoes play,
Each petal tells a tale of day.
Whispers of laughter, echoes of sighs,
Time dances gently 'neath painted skies.

Faded photographs line the walls,
Sunlight filters through the calls.
Fragrant memories linger here,
Softened edges, held so near.

The rustling leaves in silent grace,
Remind me of a sweet embrace.
Moments captured, never lost,
In the warmth, we count the cost.

Beneath the arch of blooming trees,
Time slows down with every breeze.
With open hearts, we gather more,
Harvesting joy from the forest floor.

In this sanctuary of dreams,
The world transforms, or so it seems.
Where memories live, forever bright,
In a petal's caress, we find our light.

Portraits of Fragrant Time

In the frames of memory's art,
Each scent whispers to the heart.
Lilies bloom in the twilight's glow,
Drawing us closer, so soft and slow.

A garden alive with vibrant hues,
Where every shade tells stories true.
The fragrance lingers in the air,
As we wander, without a care.

Time retreats in gentle waves,
Each moment, a treasure that saves.
Like portraits hung in galleries fine,
Moments captured, forever shine.

Amongst the petals, stories bloom,
Filling spaces where shadows loom.
With every breath, we dive deep,
Into fragrant memories we keep.

Golden hours blend and sway,
In the tapestry of day.
Through portraits of time, we find our way,
Colors of the heart forever stay.

Eternal Resonance in Lavender Whispers

In fields where lavender dreams align,
The whispers of the past entwine.
Echoes drift on the softest breeze,
A song of peace that seeks to please.

Each bloom a note in the silent air,
Resonating with love and care.
As twilight descends, shadows dance,
In lavender's embrace, we find our chance.

Remembered laughter fills the night,
Under the stars, so pure and bright.
Moments hover like delicate chimes,
Carried softly through endless times.

In the stillness where we lay,
The world fades softly away.
Wrapped in fragrance, all is clear,
Lavender whispers, drawing near.

The heart remembers, never forgets,
In dreams, we weave our silhouettes.
In eternal resonance, we find grace,
With lavender's whisper, our secret place.

A Tapestry of Blooming Echoes

In the weavings of a fragrant tale,
Echoes bloom through every trail.
Colors merge in a vibrant song,
Where heartbeats and petals belong.

Threads of time are gently spun,
A tapestry woven under the sun.
Each stitch a moment, cherished and bright,
In a dance of shadows and radiant light.

Among the flowers, laughter plays,
Moments captured in sweet arrays.
Petals fall like dreams on the ground,
In each echo, love is found.

With every breeze, a memory stirs,
In the garden where the heart concurs.
A blooming echo, a fragrant scent,
In the tapestry of life, so well spent.

Together we wander, hand in hand,
Through blooming echoes of this land.
Where the past and present intertwine,
Creating a legacy divine.

The Unbroken Cycle of Nature's Art

In the heart of the green, life begins anew,
Each blossom a promise, each leaf a hue.
Whispers of winds dance through the trees,
Nature's canvas alive, swaying with ease.

From seed to sprout, the journey unfolds,
The stories of seasons in silence told.
With rain's soft caress and sun's warm glow,
The cycle persists, forever to grow.

Mountains stand tall, while rivers entwine,
A testament clear of a grand design.
With every sunset, the stars take their flight,
Nature's art framed in the blanket of night.

In patterns of seasons, we find our place,
Connected in rhythm, a sacred embrace.
The unbroken cycle, a dance so divine,
Crafted by forces beyond the confine.

May we cherish, protect, and hold dear,
For nature's art flourishes when we revere.
In every breath, in the rustle and sigh,
The unbroken cycle, our spirits rely.

Rhapsody of Sun-Drenched Petals

In gardens of gold where the sunlight spills,
Petals awaken, time gently thrills.
Blossoms embrace the warmth of the day,
Nature's sweet melody, in fragrance they sway.

With colors that sing beneath azure skies,
They dance in the breeze with joyful goodbyes.
Each bloom tells a story, a moment in time,
In rhapsodies whispered, as life starts to rhyme.

Dew-kissed in morn, with the dawning light,
They revel in glory, a glorious sight.
In their petals lies magic, a spark of delight,
A symphony woven from day into night.

As shadows grow long, and daylight will fade,
The petals surrender in twilight's parade.
Yet in their slumber, new dreams will arise,
In the rhapsody sung beneath moonlit skies.

Through seasons they dance, though the years may change,
Each sun-drenched moment feels wondrous and strange.
The rhapsody flows as the heart softly beats,
In the tapestry woven, love infinitely seats.

The Gentle Tears of a Morning Dew

Softly they glisten on blades of green,
The morning dew, a sight serene.
Whispers of night still linger near,
Gentle tears that the dawn holds dear.

Each droplet a jewel, a fleeting grace,
Caught in the light, nature's embrace.
They cradle the world in delicate hues,
As whispers of sunlight begin to infuse.

From garden to wild, where glories unfold,
The soft tears shimmer like stories untold.
Life's quiet beginnings in silence appear,
Glistening softly, drawing us near.

But with the sun's rise, they bid their goodbye,
Fading like dreams as the moments slip by.
Yet in their passing, a promise remains,
New morns will come, and with them, new gains.

In the cycle of life, with each dawn anew,
We celebrate softly the gentle dew.
For every tear that the dawn will bestow,
Is a gift of tomorrow, a chance to grow.

An Ode to the Unfading Blossom

In gardens of wonder, where colors entwine,
There blooms a rare blossom, steadfast and fine.
Unfading in beauty, through trials it stands,
A testament strong of nature's commands.

With petals unfurling in grace and delight,
It dances with shadows, a dance full of light.
Beneath the vast heavens, in sunlight's warm glow,
An ode to the blossom, forever to grow.

Seasons may change, and the winds may shift,
Yet in its deep roots, the spirit won't drift.
With resilience woven in each gentle fold,
The story of strength is quietly told.

The fragrance it bears, a love song once sung,
A chorus of nature where hope is still young.
An unfading promise, against the decay,
In the heart of each bloom, a vow to stay.

So let us be mindful of beauty we find,
In blossoms that flourish, in petals aligned.
An ode to the unfading, through all that we face,
In nature's own art, we discover our place.

Threads of Nature's Memory

In the quiet woods, time stands still,
Whispers of leaves, a gentle thrill.
Roots entwined in the earth's warm glow,
Echoes of stories, we long to know.

Beneath the sky, clouds softly drift,
Carving the air with nature's gift.
Streams murmur secrets, old and wise,
Reflecting the dance of the sunlit skies.

Petals unfurl, colors so bright,
Painting the day, fading to night.
Each moment captured, like dew on a rose,
In nature's embrace, our heartbeats pulse.

Through seasons' change, life intertwines,
A tapestry woven, the heart defines.
In the fragrance of pine, memories sway,
Nature's whispers guide us, come what may.

From mountain peaks to valleys low,
In every breath, the wonders flow.
In the quietest corners, find the trace,
Of life's sweet journey, a gentle embrace.

The Age-Old Blossom's Secret

In the garden's heart, blooms a tale,
Petals unfold, where dreams prevail.
A fragrant history, whispered low,
Of love and longing, we yearn to know.

Twilight brings shadows, soft and deep,
Promising secrets that flowers keep.
Beneath the moon, in silver light,
Blossoms share their magic with the night.

With each sunrise, new life begins,
A dance of colors, where time spins.
Bees hum their tunes, a delicate song,
In nature's embrace, we all belong.

The rustling blooms tell tales of old,
Of passion and pain, in petals bold.
Every fragrance a memory sealed,
In the age-old tales, our hearts are healed.

So pause beneath the flowering trees,
Listen closely to the sighing breeze.
For in each blossom, a story flows,
An age-old secret that nature knows.

Scented Memories in the Breeze

The winds carry notes of days gone by,
Whispers of laughter, a soft goodbye.
Each breath of air holds a fragrant trace,
Of moments cherished, lost in space.

Marigolds bloom, their orange bright,
Stirring the heart with pure delight.
Lilacs sway in hues of soft dreams,
Fleeting moments, or so it seems.

A hint of lavender curls through the trees,
Wrapped in stories that drift on the breeze.
Sweet jasmine lingers in twilight's glance,
Inviting the past to a wistful dance.

Faded sunflowers nod as they sway,
A memory's echo, come what may.
In the gentle brush of a summer's night,
The scent of the earth feels pure and right.

Hold close the scent of those fleeting hours,
The whispers of blossoms, the laughter of flowers.
In the breeze, let the memories tease,
A fragrant reminder of life's sweet ease.

Radiance of the Unfading Flower

In gardens lush, where blossoms bloom,
Resilience thrives, dispelling gloom.
Petals aglow with radiant hue,
A testament to life, forever new.

Against the storms, they brave the night,
Drawing strength from an inner light.
Golden sunflowers reach for the dawn,
In the dance of life, they farewell the fawn.

With every petal, a story is spun,
Of battles fought and victories won.
Through seasons' change, their spirits rise,
Unfading beauty beneath vast skies.

In twilight's embrace, a flicker remains,
Hope blooms eternal, despite the chains.
Each flower a beacon, in shades so bright,
Igniting the dark with wondrous light.

So let us wander where blossoms stay,
In nature's mirror, we'll find our way.
For in their presence, we find our power,
In their radiance, life's unfading flower.

The Dance of Colors Through Seasons

In spring, blossoms bloom bright,
A canvas of pink and white.
Summer brings emerald hues,
Beneath skies of endless blues.

Autumn paints with fiery grace,
Leaves turn gold in their embrace.
Winter whispers, cold and clear,
A tapestry of white appears.

Each season holds a story told,
In shades so vivid, rich, and bold.
Nature dances, ever rare,
In cycles spinning through the air.

From dawn till dusk, colors shift,
Each moment a precious gift.
In this dance of time and space,
Life unfolds in vibrant grace.

Let us cherish every stage,
Turn the leaf, and turn the page.
In the dance of colors bright,
Find the beauty, pure delight.

Resonance in Nature's Palette

Colors speak in softest tones,
Where the river gently moans.
Verdant green and sky so blue,
Nature's art, forever true.

Crimson blossoms grace the field,
Golden grains, their wealth revealed.
The rustling leaves, a whispered sound,
In harmony, life is found.

Mountains rise, their peaks adorned,
In twilight's glow, the sky warmed.
Each hue a note in nature's song,
A symphony where we belong.

Morning light brings forth the gold,
Stories of the earth retold.
In shades of dusk, the day departs,
Nature speaks to longing hearts.

Embrace the colors that we see,
In every hue, a memory.
Resonance in each distinctive shade,
In the palette, dreams are made.

In the Embrace of Leaf and Time

The gentle rustle of the leaf,
Carries tales of joy and grief.
In its veins, history flows,
Whispers of what nature knows.

As the sun drapes gold at noon,
Life awakens, sings a tune.
The shadows stretch, then softly fade,
In the dance of light and shade.

Seasons shape each verdant edge,
Time unfolds the mystic pledge.
In stillness, find what nature gives,
In each moment, truly lives.

A leaf may fall, its journey done,
Yet in the earth, it's never gone.
It feeds the roots, the cycle's spin,
In the embrace, life begins again.

Nature holds us close and tight,
In her arms, we find the light.
Through each bend and twist of fate,
We learn to love, we learn to wait.

The Everlasting Tale of a Simple Bud

A simple bud on boughs does grow,
In silent grace, it steals the show.
With tender petals, it will unfold,
A story of beauty to be told.

The dew of dawn, a crystal kiss,
Awakens dreams in morning's bliss.
As sunlight warms the gentle bloom,
It chases shadows, banishes gloom.

With every breeze that comes to pass,
The bud unveils its vibrant class.
In colors deep, it finds its voice,
In every hue, the heart's rejoice.

Though seasons change and days may wane,
The bud stands firm through sun and rain.
A testament to strength and grace,
In quiet courage, it finds its place.

The world may rush, but here it stays,
A symphony of simple ways.
In every bloom, a tale replete,
Of moments cherished, bittersweet.

Whispers of Timeless Bloom

In the garden where shadows play,
Petals unfold, revealing day.
Voices of the earth softly weave,
Secrets of a world, hard to believe.

Morning dew, a crystal sigh,
Kissing leaves where dreams lie.
Nature's song, a tender call,
Echoing love in the stillness of all.

Time drips slow like waxen flame,
Each moment whispers a name.
Breezes dance through tangled vines,
In every rustle, life entwines.

Colors blend in a soft embrace,
Painting joy upon nature's face.
Underneath the sky so wide,
Whispers bloom like secrets tied.

Evening falls with gentle grace,
Stars awaken, a sacred space.
In the stillness, dreams take flight,
Guided by the silver light.

Fragrance of Infinite Moments

Scented air in a twilight glow,
Cascades of fragrance ebb and flow.
Each whiff a tale, a memory,
Lingering softly, forever free.

Through the fields where wildflowers sway,
Time stretches thin, like sun's last ray.
A whisper of amaryllis blooms,
Filling hearts with sweet perfumes.

In every petal, stories hide,
Of laughter shared and tears cried.
Moments woven in nature's thread,
Awakening dreams, softly spread.

As twilight mingles with the night,
Stars ignite, a guiding light.
Reminders of love, sweet and pure,
In fragrance, we find the cure.

Together we chase the fading sun,
In every scent, our souls are one.
Winds carry whispers through the trees,
Fragrance of moments, forever frees.

Echoes of a Blossoming Heart

In the silence where hearts reside,
Echoes of love, like a rising tide.
Whispers twine through fragile blooms,
Bringing light to shadowed rooms.

Petals unfold with a gentle grace,
Embracing the warmth of love's embrace.
Every heartbeat, a rhythmic song,
A journey where we all belong.

In gardens lush with hues so bright,
Colors dance in the fading light.
Tender moments carved in time,
Each breath a soft, gentle rhyme.

As daylight fades, the stars unite,
Guiding dreams into the night.
In the quiet, feelings stir,
Echoes of love that always were.

A canvas painted with desire,
Each stroke igniting passion's fire.
In every bloom, a story's part,
The endless echoes of a heart.

Dance of Lasting Flora

Among the petals, dances grace,
Life's sweet rhythm in a sacred space.
Nature sways in vibrant hues,
A tapestry of ancient cues.

Leaves flutter like whispers of fate,
Every movement, a song innate.
Twilight glimmers on the dawn,
In this dance, we are reborn.

Time suspends as flowers spin,
A timeless waltz where dreams begin.
Underneath the moon's soft gaze,
Every step a gentle phase.

Laughter weaves through fragrant air,
In the dance, we shed our care.
Harmony sings through every bloom,
Chasing shadows, dispelling gloom.

Boundless blossoms, hand in hand,
We twirl through life, a merry band.
In the garden where love thrives,
Dance with me, where magic drives.

Petal by Petal

Softly they fall from the tree,
Glistening like tears of the sky.
Each petal whispers of love,
In colors that dance and fly.

Beneath the warm glow of the sun,
They carpet the earth with grace.
In every hue and each shade,
Nature finds its embrace.

As breezes carry them far,
To places we cannot see,
They journey on silent paths,
In a flight so wild and free.

In stillness, they rest on the ground,
Creating a quilt of delight.
A reminder that beauty fades,
Yet lingers in memory's light.

Petal by petal, we learn,
The transient nature of life.
In each moment, we gather,
Love blooms amid joy and strife.

Time Flows

Time wanders like a gentle stream,
Carving the banks of our days.
Each moment fleeting, yet profound,
Moments lost in the sun's rays.

The past is a whisper behind,
Echoes of laughter and tears.
It shapes the contours of our dreams,
Woven through shadows of years.

Like a river, it will not cease,
Moving through valleys and hills.
In the stillness, we ponder deep,
As time with quiet grace fills.

We chase the clocks as they tick,
Holding on to what soon must fade.
Yet in each heartbeat, we find,
The treasures that memories made.

Time flows like the tides of the sea,
Endlessly shifting and new.
In its current, we find our place,
Embracing what life will construe.

Heartbeats in a Sea of Blossoms

Amidst the blooms, our hearts align,
Each pulse a note in spring's song.
In vibrant gardens, we discover,
A rhythm where we both belong.

Petals dance in the soft breeze,
Swaying to nature's sweet tune.
The fragrance of love fills the air,
Under the warm glow of the moon.

With every heartbeat, a promise,
Life blooms in passion and grace.
In the tapestry of petals,
Love writes its own tender space.

We wander through fields of color,
Lost in the beauty we share.
In silence, our souls intertwine,
We breathe in the sweet, fragrant air.

Heartbeats echo in the still night,
Where blossoms pulse with delight.
In this garden of whispered dreams,
Love blossoms, forever bright.

The Merging Tides of Floral Memories

In the garden, memories linger,
Each flower a tale of our past.
Soft whispers of laughter and love,
In petals, our stories are cast.

Tides of time wash over us,
In hues of both joy and pain.
With every bloom, we journey back,
To moments cherished, not in vain.

The rich scent of nostalgia breathes,
Transporting us to those days.
Where sunshine kissed our dreams awake,
And hearts danced in luminous sways.

As seasons change, so do we,
Yet bonds of love remain true.
In every leaf and every stem,
Floral memories guide us through.

Merging tides of laughter and tears,
Painting our lives with grace flows.
In the symphony of color and light,
Our hearts blossom, forever grows.

Luminescence of the Unyielding Bud

In darkness, the bud dares to bloom,
Reaching for light with fierce resolve.
A promise of beauty held tight,
In silence, life's mysteries evolve.

With morning's dew, it awakens,
A dance with the sun on its face.
The struggles it faced as it grew,
Bring forth a courage and grace.

Colors burst forth in brilliance,
A testament to the fight.
In the heart of the softly unyielding,
Lives a spirit that's radiant, bright.

Each petal unfurls with a purpose,
A story entwined with the day.
In every fragile unfolding,
Strength finds its own unique way.

Luminescence captures our eyes,
As nature's symphony plays.
In the heart of every small bud,
Lies a light that forever stays.

Guardians of the Floral Horizon

In the morning light they sway,
Petals bright in soft array,
Watchers of the world anew,
Guardians clad in every hue.

Beneath the sky, they stand so tall,
Their fragrance whispers, beckons all,
With each breeze, secrets unfold,
Stories of the brave and bold.

In the dusk, they hold their grace,
In twilight's warm and soft embrace,
Keeping vigil, through the night,
Underneath the stars' soft light.

Through storms and sun, they bend, yet thrive,
Roots run deep, they stay alive,
In the garden, life persists,
Nature's magic, none can resist.

Guardians here, forever seen,
In hues of gold and vibrant green,
A testament to time and space,
In every petal, love and grace.

What Remains in the Bloom's Silhouette

Shadows cast by summer's sun,
Where the timeless blooms have spun,
Echoes linger, soft and clear,
Memories of those held dear.

In the petals, whispers dwell,
Stories that they have to tell,
Underneath the fading light,
A silhouette, dark and bright.

Seasons change, yet still they stand,
Carving traces in the sand,
A dance between the dusk and dawn,
In every bloom, a thread is drawn.

What remains when all is lost?
Beauty still, no matter cost,
In the heart, the essence stays,
In the bloom's lasting gaze.

Fragments of a life once kissed,
In the garden, they exist,
What remains in colors bold,
Treasures in the tales retold.

The Silence of Enduring Blooms

Amidst the chaos, silent they stand,
Nature's canvas, finely planned,
In soft hues, they meet the day,
A stillness that won't go away.

Whispers ride on gentle air,
In the garden, peace laid bare,
Enduring blooms in quiet gleam,
Holding tight a waking dream.

Time flows gently, never rush,
In their presence, heartbeats hush,
A lullaby in every leaf,
A treasure found beyond belief.

In their stillness, truths reside,
Innocence, a timeless guide,
With each bloom, a breath, a sigh,
A promise of the days gone by.

The silence speaks, transcends the sound,
In every flower, peace is found,
The enduring blooms softly embrace,
A sacred truth in nature's grace.

Celestial Dance of Nature's Finery

Underneath the vast expanse,
Nature holds a mystic dance,
Stars align, the earth takes flight,
In the blooms, purest light.

Petals twirl in moonlit waltz,
In the breeze, no sign of faults,
Dainty twirls, a cosmic sigh,
Hearts awakened, spirits high.

Each color sings, a gentle song,
In this dance, where all belong,
The fragrance lifts, a sweet perfume,
In every corner, life will bloom.

As dawn unfolds its tender face,
Nature whispers, finds its place,
The celestial dance won't cease,
In every bloom, we find our peace.

Through the seasons, rhythms flow,
In harmony, the blossoms glow,
Nature weaves its story fine,
In the dance of life's design.

The Everlasting Floral Dance

In the garden where colors sway,
Petals twirl in the bright ballet.
Nature's rhythm, a sweet romance,
In the breeze, they spin and prance.

Morning dew on leaves aglow,
Whispers soft that ebb and flow.
Every blossom tells a tale,
In the wind, their voices sail.

Fragrant scents in gentle air,
Capturing hearts with tender care.
A union of shades, bold and bright,
Guided by soft moon's light.

Time stands still in this embrace,
Every flower finds its place.
As seasons change, they still shall dance,
In eternal bliss, a chance.

Nature's love, forever true,
In every shade and every hue.
With every bloom, the world enchants,
In the everlast floral dance.

Echoes of a Wondrous Blossom

In the silence, blooms arise,
Crafting beauty, under skies.
Echoes whisper, softly stay,
As daylight fades to twilight's play.

Petals brush against the night,
In their glow, there's pure delight.
Secrets nestled in each hold,
Stories of the brave and bold.

Time cascades, as flowers sigh,
Beneath the watchful stars up high.
In each fold, a dream takes flight,
Echoes of the wondrous light.

In the garden, heartbeats blend,
Every blossom, a cherished friend.
Nature weaves, with gentle hands,
Creating worlds where love expands.

So linger here, let shadows pass,
In the whispers, find your glass.
For in the petals, life is spun,
Echoes of the bloom, it's won.

Serene Essence of Forever

In morning light, the world awakes,
   Softly breathing, as it shakes.
   Whispers of the dawn arise,
   Serene essence fills the skies.

Feathered friends begin to sing,
Nature's song, the heart will cling.
   Flora bows with gentle grace,
   In this peaceful, sacred space.

Waves of color, pure delight,
Kissing shadows, chasing light.
   In the garden, time shall bend,
   Moments lost, yet never end.

Quiet chambers hold the dreams,
   In a dance of sunlit beams.
Each petal's touch, a soft caress,
Radiates the warmth of blessedness.

So breathe in deep, and hold it near,
   In every heartbeat, love appears.
   For in the garden, life's a tether,
   To the serene essence of forever.

In the Garden of Endless Love

Where the sun kisses the earth,
Blossoms bloom, proclaim their worth.
In the garden, hearts unite,
Under stars, in the soft light.

Whispers echo, sweet and clear,
In each petal, love draws near.
Fragrant hues entwined above,
Painting skies with endless love.

Each moment feels like a dream,
Lost in nature's gentle scheme.
Dancing shadows, hand in hand,
In this realm, our hearts will stand.

Seasons change, yet still remain,
In our souls, the love we gain.
Every flower tells a story,
In the garden, find our glory.

So let the blooms forever sway,
In this love, we'll find our way.
With every breath, we'll rise above,
In the garden of endless love.

Shadows of Tomorrow's Garden

In whispers soft, the shadows grow,
As twilight dances, secrets flow.
Each leaf a tale, each stem a dream,
In this lush realm, we softly gleam.

The moonlight weaves through tangled vines,
Revealing hope where darkness twines.
Beneath the stars, the futures lie,
In the garden's heart, we softly sigh.

With every rustle, old ghosts stir,
In fragrant blooms, their stories blur.
They guide the heart, a gentle hand,
Through echoes lost in time's vast land.

The petals shimmer, kissed by night,
In shadows cast, we find our light.
Each moment held within the leaves,
A tapestry, our heart's reprieves.

So let us wander through this hue,
Where shadows dance and dreams renew.
For in tomorrow's garden fair,
We plant our hopes, our love laid bare.

Carried by the Winds of Heritage

Across the fields, the whispers fly,
Of ancient tales that never die.
Each echo sings of lessons earned,
In every heart, the fires burned.

The winds that blow through aged trees,
Tell stories wrapped in gentle breeze.
Of hands once clasped in unity,
A bond that breathes in you and me.

Roots delve deep in rich, dark soil,
Through storms endured and sacred toil.
In every leaf, a voice persists,
Inheritances through fog and mist.

From distant lands, our spirits roam,
In shared laughter, we find our home.
As rivers merge, our paths entwine,
In heritage, our souls align.

So let the winds of old embrace,
The beauty found in every grace.
Together, we will rise and soar,
Carried by winds forevermore.

Crossing Paths with Timeless Flora

In every step, a bloom appears,
A tapestry of hopes and fears.
Through winding trails, we find our way,
Where timeless flora dare to play.

The daisies nod with gentle smiles,
In gardens vast, across the miles.
Their colors clash, yet harmonize,
In nature's art, a sweet surprise.

Beneath the boughs of ancient trees,
The whispers weave with summer's breeze.
Their roots entwined in rich embrace,
In every shade, a sacred space.

Through fragrant meadows, we will stride,
Where dreams and blossoms coincide.
And as we pause, the world shall crack,
With petals soft, we'll not look back.

For in this place, we come alive,
With every leaf, our spirits thrive.
Crossing paths with nature's song,
In timeless flora, we belong.

When Petals Write Their Legends

In gardens vast, the stories bloom,
As petals swirl, dispelling gloom.
Each hue a chapter, bright and bold,
A legacy in colors told.

The roses speak of love's sweet pain,
The lilacs whisper joy and rain.
From every stem, a tale will rise,
In nature's book, where truth defies.

The gentle fall of softest sighs,
In every fragrance, hope complies.
As each petal drifts upon the breeze,
A legend grows among the trees.

When morning light begins to crest,
The blooms awake, in sunlight dressed.
With every dawn, a new refrain,
A story etched in joy and pain.

So let us wander through this place,
Where petals write with gentle grace.
In gardens rich with tales divine,
A legend lives, forever mine.